JUST IN TIME!

ADVENT SERVICES

David G. Rogne

Abingdon Press
Nashville

JUST IN TIME!
ADVENT SERVICES

This book is printed on acid-free paper.

Library of Congress Cataloging-in-Publication Data

Rogne, David George, 1934-
Advent services / David G. Rogne.
p. cm. — (Just in time!)
Includes bibliographical references and index.
ISBN-13: 978-0-687-46581-1 (binding: pbk., adhesive, perfect : alk. paper)
1. Advent. I. Title. II. Series: Just in time! (Nashville, Tenn.)

BV40.R64 2007
264—dc22

2006017380

07 08 09 10 11 12 13 14 15 16—10 9 8 7 6 5 4 3 2 1
MANUFACTURED IN THE UNITED STATES OF AMERICA

This is for

Seth, Ian, Micaela,

Olivia, and Turner

CONTENTS

INTRODUCTION

My grandchildren like to curl up on my lap to have me read a story that has been read to them hundreds of times. They know all the characters, and know what each is going to say. They know the story so well they can pretend to read by looking at the pictures. My grandchilren like what is familiar, but it doesn't challenge them to live differently. They can tell the story by heart without ever making application to themselves.

For those preachers who follow the lectionary, Advent and Christmas can send us back over the same ground that we have been plowing for years. Perhaps the "old, old story" never grows old, but when we have been telling it for years, it becomes increasingly difficult to find ways to challenge the congregation to hear it in a new way that will call for response. They know the characters by heart, but their very familiarity with the story may prevent them from asking, "What does this mean for me?"

There is a poetic adage that says, "Though Christ a thousand times in Bethlehem be born, if he is not born in thee, thy soul is still forlorn." The purpose of the messages and materials in this book is to encourage people to look at some of the ways we describe the one whose coming we celebrate in this season and to ask what each of those descriptions means for our conduct.

First Sunday of Advent

Ways We Know Him: Emmanuel

Scripture: Isaiah 7:14

Sermon

Seven hundred years before Christ, the prophet Isaiah was trying to convince his king to trust in God rather than in foreign alliances. When the king remained unconvinced, the prophet told him that, as a sign of God's trustworthiness, a child would be born to an undesignated young woman. Before the child became old enough to distinguish between right and wrong, the nations that the king now feared would be destroyed. The child's name would reflect Isaiah's message; he would be called *Emmanuel*, which means "God is with us." Undoubtedly, such a child was born. Whether he had any significance for the king, we do not know. But even if he did, it was not enduring.

Seven centuries later, Jesus was born in Bethlehem. When his disciple, Matthew, sought to record the significance of Jesus' coming, he turned back to the words of Isaiah and suggested that these words were more adequately fulfilled by Jesus than by anyone in the days of the prophet. From that time to this, *Emmanuel*,

"God is with us," has stood for what Christians have felt happened at that first Christmas; that somehow, in Jesus, God was incarnated among us, took on human flesh and blood. But what does it mean to us? Perhaps the very title, Emmanuel, can shed some light.

Emmanuel—God Is with Us

For one thing, to call Jesus Emmanuel is to say something about God: that God is with us, not against us. This is consistent with what the Bible has always taught about God. We read that somewhere back in the dawn of time, God created human beings in order to have fellowship with them. Because of human pride and self-sufficiency, the relationship was strained and human beings wandered away from the relationship for which they were made. God has made numerous attempts to call God's children back to their destiny, but they keep losing the way. The stars, the mountains, the trees all testify to God's greatness, but humans have bowed before these things and worshiped them instead of the Creator. God sent Moses with laws that were intended to show that life is ethical, but instead of learning how to live as children of God, people have made a fetish out of the law, attempting to keep the letter, but missing the spirit. God sent prophets to guide people back to God. They taught that God did not desire ritual or ceremony, but justice, mercy, humility, and sincerity. Many of the prophets were killed for their efforts.

Still, God was determined not to give up. In the person of Jesus, God attempted to make it plain to us that God is among us, not as accuser, not as judge, not as punisher, but as love. God became involved with people in such a way that they couldn't miss the fact that he cared. Jesus didn't just preach about leprosy;

he touched the leper in love. He didn't just give a lecture on hunger; he fed those whose stomachs were empty. He didn't merely talk about lingering loneliness; he went to people's homes and sat down for supper and an evening chat.

Charles Wesley, in his struggle to find salvation, envisioned himself as Jacob, wrestling with some unknown and malignant spirit in the desert. Then, Wesley discovered that the one he had been wrestling with was none other than God. In his great hymn "Come, O Thou Traveler Unknown" originally entitled, "Wrestling Jacob," Wesley wrote:

> 'Tis Love! 'tis Love! Thou diedst for me,
> I hear thy whisper in my heart.
> The morning breaks, the shadows flee,
> pure Universal Love thou art.
> To me, to all, my mercy's move;
> thy nature, and thy name is Love.

That love still liberates us today. Toyohiko Kagawa, that great Japanese Christian, has said what a great discovery it was for him. In *Meditations* (New York: Harper and Row, 1950) he writes that he grew up as a frightened child in Japan because he was told that there were evil spirits everywhere, and that they would damn him for the slightest misdeed. He felt that there was nowhere in the universe where he could find love and affection. When he was introduced to the Christian faith he was overwhelmed and relieved to be told that the essence of the universe is love and that God is a loving father. For him, the good news of Jesus was the assurance that at the center of the universe is a loving creator. For him, that was the power of Christianity.

In Christ, God pierces our defenses, and says, "Emmanuel—God is with us."

Emmanuel—God Is with Us

To call Jesus Emmanuel not only says something about God, but about Jesus. When we say that God is with us, we are being reminded that Jesus is contemporary. Of course, Jesus was an historical human being. He had a normal body like ours, familiar with weariness, hunger, thirst, pleasure, suffering, and death. His emotional life was a normal human life like our own. He was at times astonished, compassionate, indignant, rejoicing, and sorrowful. His mental life was normal and human like our own. He learned from observation, he learned to read and write, "Jesus grew in wisdom and stature," says Luke (2:52 NIV). There was humanness in his spiritual life. He prayed, not as though he were God, but as though he were human, sometimes triumphantly, sometimes seeking strength. The reason for listing these indications of Jesus' humanity is simply to remind us that, whatever else he was, Jesus was human. Sometimes, in our efforts to keep Jesus unique, we are tempted to accentuate his divinity, and in so doing, lose sight of his humanity.

However, to affirm that Jesus was an historical person does not necessarily ensure a vital Christian faith. The Jesus of history lived a long time ago, and for many, that relegates him to the past, along with King Arthur and other noble persons of antiquity. Many people will observe Christmas this year, but the coming of Jesus will have no personal significance for them.

For Christ to matter, there must be something contemporary about him, and there is. In his life on earth Jesus said, "Whoever believes in me believes not in me but in him who sent me" (John 12:44). "I am the gate," he said (John 10:9), but we don't stop at the gate: we go through it to what it leads to. "I am the way," he said (John 14:6), but we don't end with the way; we go along it to what it arrives at. So Jesus saw his own significance, not simply in the life he lived two thousand years ago, but in terms of the everlasting presence of God he came to proclaim.

That presence is with us today. Our problem is that we often miss it. A young father's conversation with his four-year-old daughter illustrates the point.

"Daddy," she said, "God is everywhere, isn't he?"

"Yes," he responded, "God is everywhere."

"Is God a spirit?"

"Yes, God is a spirit."

"We can't see spirits, can we?"

"No, we can't."

"Well, what I don't understand is, if God is everywhere and we can't see God; how come we aren't bumping into him all the time?" (story attributed to Richard K. Wallarab, 1988).

The tragedy is that we are constantly bumping into God, but we don't realize it. In the neighbor in need, in the lost, in the lonely and broken, God reaches out to us, but in our self-concern we don't respond to God's touch.

For many, that presence has become more visible in Jesus. After a lifetime of struggle, controversies, and family problems, John Wesley, the founder of Methodism, lay on his deathbed, contemplating the continuing presence and love of God as he had experienced it in Christ. As he lay dying, he said: "The best of all is, God is with us" (quoted in Jerry L. Mercer, *Follow the Star: A Study Book* [Nashville: Graded Press, 1983], 34).

And it isn't just people of the past who have discovered that. In a book entitled *Zapped by Jesus*, Jeannette Struchen quotes a young person:

"The new way of livin' is with you, Jesus. You're what's happening. For the first time in my life I'm ten feet tall, you know. I'm not a phony, Jesus, I'm alive and lusty because you're alive and lusty and expect me to be too . . . You've given me guts to face myself and dared me to stop coppin' out and thinkin' I had answers. Man, you're the answer. The only answer. Hallelujah, Jesus! What a surprise you turned out to be."

Emmanuel—not "God was with us," but "God is with us."

Emmanuel—God Is With Us

To call Jesus *Emmanuel* is to say something not only about God and about Jesus, but about us, for it means that God is *with* us. "Jesus is what God means by humanity; Jesus is what humanity means by God" (attributed to F. W. Boreham). The architect finds expression in granite; the artist finds expression in paint; the author seeks expression in print; but God chose to find expression in a human being.

I do not know how God filled Jesus of Nazareth, but a colleague has given me a meaningful analogy. He was sitting at his desk trying to come up with something that would help people to understand the incarnation. His leather gloves, which he had thrown on his desk, caught his attention. They were limp and lifeless. He reached over, picked one up, and slipped his hand into it. The glove filled out. He flexed his hand and the glove moved. It was filled with life. His mind began to dance with the thought of God coming to earth to slip into the glove of a human life. God was at work in Jesus as a hand in a glove, so that by looking at the actions of Jesus, we may get an idea of the actions of God.

But there is more to it. Gloves come in pairs. We are the other glove. God seeks to dwell in us also. If we wonder how God-filled people are supposed to act, we have been given Jesus as an example. Martin Luther called us "little Christs" (as quoted by John and Barbara Brokhoff in *Faith Alive!* [Lima, Ohio: C.S.S., 1978], 77).

When Mahatma Gandhi, who had once been turned away from a Christian church because of the color of his skin, was asked how Christians could best carry out their work in India, he suggested that Christians begin by living more like Christ. He urged Christians to put their emphasis on love, for love is the soul of Christianity. If Christians would do that, he said, they would succeed.

In order to make that love concrete, God came among us, filled the humanity of Jesus, and enlisted us in his cause. "You're Christ to me," cried a dying soldier to Florence Nightingale in the Crimea as she went around the yard at night, carrying her lamp. "You're Christ to me"; then he fell back and died (as quoted by James S. Stewart in *River of Life* [Nashville: Parthenon Press, 1972], 91). People in whom God dwells are to act like Jesus.

God Is with Us

I close with this. It was Christmas Eve. A man was sitting in his easy chair enjoying a warm fire. His wife had asked him to go with her to the Christmas Eve service in the village church. "No," he replied. "It would be hypocritical of me to go when I don't believe in that stuff." So his wife went without him. As he sat reflecting, the wind began to pick up velocity and snow began to swirl. Suddenly, he was startled by several thumps against the living room window. He jumped up and looked out into the storm. On the ground in front of the window he saw three little birds, lying dazed. He then saw many birds perched on the bushes, shivering in the winter storm. Thinking about their plight, he put on his coat and boots and went outside to see if he could help. He decided to open the barn door, so that the birds could roost in its shelter for the night. But the birds wouldn't trust him. When he went toward them, they hopped away. Again and again he tried to catch them, but they hopped out of reach. "If only I could catch them," he thought, "I could put them in the warm barn where they could stay for the night." But all his attempts were futile. He dashed back into the house and got a few pieces of bread, hoping to make a path of crumbs, which might lead the birds to the barn. But the birds would have nothing to do with his effort to save them. He felt helpless to convey his concern for them. "If only I could become one of them," he thought in his desperation, "then I could show them the way." At that moment, the church bells rang wildly from the village church. It was midnight. The bells were announcing that it was Christmas Day, the celebration of *Emmanuel*—God is with us. Suddenly, everything the man had heard about Christmas fell into place. Out of compassion for a confused and erring race, God had found a way to contact humans: by becoming one of them.

Emmanuel—God is with us. God has been with us all along. In so many ways, God has tried to tell us. In Jesus, God has come to show us. Through us, God seeks to show the world.

Old Testament Lesson

Isaiah 7:10-14

Again the LORD spoke to Ahaz, saying, Ask a sign of the LORD your God; let it be deep as Sheol or high as heaven. But Ahaz said, I will not ask, and I will not put the LORD to the test. Then Isaiah said: "Hear then, O house of David! Is it too little for you to weary mortals, that you weary my God also? Therefore the Lord himself will give you a sign. Look, the young woman is with child and shall bear a son, and shall name him Immanuel.

New Testament Lesson

Matthew 1:18-23

Now the birth of Jesus the Messiah took place in this way. When his mother Mary had been engaged to Joseph, but before they lived together, she was found to be with child from the Holy Spirit. Her husband Joseph, being a righteous man and unwilling to expose her to public disgrace, planned to dismiss her quietly. But just when he had resolved to do this, an angel of the Lord appeared to him in a dream and said, "Joseph, son of David, do not be afraid to take Mary as your wife, for the child conceived in her is from the Holy Spirit. She will bear a son, and you are to name him Jesus, for he will save his people from their sins." All this took place to fulfill what had been spoken by the Lord through the prophet: "Look, the virgin shall conceive and bear a son, and they shall name him Emmanuel," which means, "God is with us."

Suggested Hymns

- "O Come, O Come, Emmanuel"
- "People, Look East"
- "Hail to the Lord's Anointed"

Pastoral Prayer

God our Creator,

We gather in the name of our Lord Jesus to learn more about him and to re-examine our lives in the light of his. May we be open to challenge, ready to confess our shortcomings, trusting in your mercy and forgiveness, and finding new life in a relationship with you that is renewed every day.

Some of us have come with worries or anxious cares, and the burden is more than we can carry. Help us to put our trust in you. Some of us have come attempting to deal with major decisions. Help us to make our decisions and then to be at peace about the choices we have made. Some of us are concerned about health—our own or that of another. We pray that health and wholeness will be our experience. Some of us are involved in a spiritual search—we are trying to discover the meaning of our lives—we are trying to become people of faith. May we find integration and satisfaction, a sense of peace and fulfillment as we learn to live life your way.

In this season of preparation, may we rediscover the promise that you are with us, and may your presence be very real. In Christ's name we pray. Amen.

Litany for Lighting the First Advent Candle

Christians around the world begin this day
to celebrate the ways in which
the coming of Christ affects our lives.
We join with them in lighting the Advent candles,
as we remind ourselves of the ways
Christ has become known to us.

We gather to celebrate the coming of Emmanuel.
The coming of Emmanuel was anticipated
from ancient times.
Our hope springs anew from an ancient vision.
Rejoice! God is with us!
As we light the first Advent candle
let it remind us that God is always present
to comfort and sustain.
May God's presence, manifested in Jesus,
be seen in us as well.

The First Advent Candle Is Lit.

Let us join our voices in singing
"Emmanuel, Emmanuel."

Second Sunday of Advent

Ways We Know Him: Son of Man

Scripture: Matthew 16:13-28

Sermon

Quite often in the Restoration plays of the seventeenth century, an author would give characters names to represent the parts they played: John Friendly, a neighbor; Dr. Serringe, a surgeon; Mrs. Callicoe, seamstress; Waitwell, a servant. This immediately conjured up identifiable images in the minds of the hearers so that the author could proceed with the play, and not have to develop every part.

Some people, even today, choose titles that conjure up certain images. One dentist in California actually changed his name to "Painless Parker," and to good advantage. In his prime, Hailie Salasie, Emperor of Ethiopia, called himself "the Lion of the Tribe of Judah" which, we must admit, gives the image of strength. Muhamed Ali, not known for his humility, called himself simply, "The Greatest."

In his day, Jesus wanted to communicate all he could about himself and his mission in as short a time as possible, so he chose for himself the title "Son of Man." What does his choice tell us?

Son of Man—Identified with Humanity

For one thing, when Jesus used the title Son of Man, he was identifying with our humanity. There have always been those who, one way or another, would deprive Jesus of his humanity. In fact, the earliest heresy the church had to deal with was not one that sought to deny his divinity, but his humanity. A group called Docetists believed that matter was evil, and that spirit was good. Because Christ was good, they taught that he could not be human—could not be made of flesh and blood. He must have been only an appearance, an apparition, a spiritual being. He was all mind, and no body. Therefore he could not suffer, he could not grow and develop, he could not die. It was because of the Docetists that the Apostles' Creed, which we recite from time to time, came to include specifics about Jesus' humanity: he was born, he suffered, he died, he was buried.

To be sure, there is a dark side to humanity, and anyone who shares that humanity is potentially flawed. I remember a conversation in which Archie Bunker, of past television fame, picked up on that idea while talking with his wife Edith.

Archie says, "That's you all right, Edith the good. You never yell. You never swear. You never make nobody mad. You think it's easy living with a saint? When you cheat you don't cheat to win. You cheat to lose. Edith, you ain't human."

Edith responds: "That's a terrible thing to say, Archie Bunker. I am just as human as you are."

"Oh, yeah," says Archie, "then prove you're just as human as me. Do something rotten."

Archie had a low view of what it means to be human.

Others have shared that low view of humanity. Friedrich Nietzsche once described humanity as but a disease on the skin of the earth. Psychoanalyst Edward Glover wrote it this way:

> The perfectly normal infant is almost completely egocentric, greedy, dirty, violent in temper, destructive in habit, profoundly sexual in purpose, aggrandizing in attitude, devoid of all but the most primitive reality sense, without conscience of moral feeling, whose attitude is . . . opportunistic, inconsiderate, domineering and sadistic . . . In fact, judged by adult social standards, the normal baby is for all practical purposes a born criminal. (*The Roots of Crime* [New York: International Universities Press, 1960], 8)

Human nature is seriously flawed.

Wanting to keep Jesus from contamination by such connections, some Christians have gone to the opposite extreme of focusing only on Jesus' perfection. They give the impression that Jesus was so different from us that he never had to make a moral decision, or if he did, it was already decided in advance that he could not sin, so his goodness is a stacked deck, his purity of life an untested virtue. If he did not have to struggle with hatred, self-indulgence, compromise, physical impulse, and ego fulfillment, then his goodness has no relevance to us, for we have to struggle with all these things. Such an understanding of Jesus turns him into a flawless piece of porcelain whose goodness is static, not growing and dynamic.

Fortunately, that is not how the New Testament paints him. The very title he chose for himself, Son of Man, is often used to demonstrate his humanity:

"The Son of Man came eating and drinking ..."
(Matthew 11:19; Luke 7:34)

"The son of man has nowhere to lay his head"
(Matthew 8:20; Luke 9:58)

"The Son of Man came not be served but to serve"
(Matthew 20:28; Mark 10:45)

"The Son of Man must undergo great suffering,
and be rejected by the elders, the chief priests,
and the scribes, and be killed."
(Mark 8:31)

"The Son of Man is going to be betrayed."
(Matthew 17:22; Luke 9:44)

Indeed, the glimpses we get of Jesus, even apart from this title, demonstrate that he was flesh and blood. He was born in Palestine of Jewish ancestry. He grew from childhood to manhood. He experienced sorrow over the death of Lazarus. He experienced anger over corrupt practices. He confessed ignorance at certain points. He demonstrated irritability.

At the very beginning of his ministry, Luke tells us that Jesus was tempted on several issues. Are we to assume that this highly stylized report is the only time Jesus was ever faced with tempting options? The writer of the letter to the Hebrews remembers Jesus differently. He says: "For we do not have a high priest who is unable to sympathize with our weaknesses, but we have one who in every respect has been tested as we are ..." (4:15). That says to me that all through life Jesus was engaged in the same kind of struggles that face us, and when he won out, it was in the same way everyone else has to. When we choose to go to him with our difficulties, we are choosing one who has been there—one who knows what it's all about. Jesus was a human being.

Son of Man—A Special Human

The second thing I want to say is that, though Jesus' use of the title Son of Man identified him as a human, it also identified him as a special human. The title Jesus chose for himself was not new. In the book of Ezekiel, written some five hundred years before Christ, the term is used some ninety times as God addresses his prophet, Ezekiel. It denotes Ezekiel's humanity, but it also has about it the status of one who is being used by God as an emissary to his people. Ezekiel, the son of man, is aware that he is a sign to his people, even as Jesus saw himself as a sign to his people.

In another Old Testament book, the book of Daniel, written some time later, there is a scene where Daniel has a dream. Kingdoms of the earth stand before him. Each one is represented by a hideous beast. The beasts devour and tear, and act without restraint. In the midst of this chaos appears one "like a son of man," (7:13 RSV) characterized by human gentleness. The *New Revised Standard Version* even translates the term as "human being."

Then again, about seventy years before Christ, *The Similitudes of Enoch* appeared. In that book, a character called the Son of Man appears as God's special agent of salvation and judgment. He is seen as a righteous man who will completely defeat the evil rulers of the world. These are the kinds of things that would have gone through people's minds when Jesus used this term. But then Jesus expanded the idea of the Son of Man.

He may have said: "Do you remember when the people of Israel were in the wilderness, and there was a snake epidemic?

Moses put a serpent on a stick and lifted it high, and all who looked to it were mysteriously healed? Do you remember that story?"

When they answered, "Yes," Jesus said, "Well, in just such a way the Son of Man must be lifted up, and all who look to him in faith will have life. And do you remember the story of Jonah?"

"Oh yes," they answered.

"Just as Jonah was three days and three nights in the belly of the sea monster, so for three days and three nights the Son of Man will be in the heart of the earth" (Matthew 12:40).

In his book *The Signature of Jesus*, Brennan Manning describes a play, "The Sign of Jonah." Hundreds of small, angry groups of people gather to wait for God's verdict at the Final Judgment.

> One group is a band of Jews . . . persecuted throughout their history. [Some of them] are victims of Nazi extermination camps . . . [They] demand to know what right God has to pass judgment on them.
>
> Another group consists of American blacks. They too question the authority of God who never has experienced the misfortunes of men, never known the squalor and depths of human degradation to which they were subjected in the suffocating holds of slave ships. A third group is composed of persons born illegitimately, the butt all their lives of jokes and sneers.
>
> Hundreds of such groups are scattered across the plain: the poor, the afflicted, the maltreated. Each group appoints a representative to . . . challenge [God's] divine right to pass sentence on their immortal destinies . . . They meet . . . and decide that this remote and distant God who never has experienced human agony is unqualified to sit in judgment unless he is willing to enter into the suffering, humiliated state of man and endure what they have undergone.
>
> Their conclusion reads: You must be born a Jew; the circumstances of your birth must be questioned; you must be

> misunderstood by everyone, insulted and mocked by your enemies, betrayed by your friends; you must be persecuted, beaten, and finally murdered in a most public and humiliating fashion.
>
> Such is the judgment passed on God by the assembly. The clamor rises to fever pitch as they await His response. Then a brilliant, dazzling light illuminates the entire plain. One by one those who have passed judgment on God fall silent. For emblazoned high in the heavens for the whole world to see is the signature of Jesus Christ with this inscription about it: I have served my sentence. (Portland, Ore.: Multnomah Press, 1992, 149–50)

When Jesus took the title Son of Man for himself, he took a recognizable and somewhat familiar term and used it in a strange new way that shocked people into listening. The Son of Man was, indeed, special, but not in the way people expected him to be.

Son of Man—Exalted Possibility

The third thing I want to say this morning is that when Jesus used the title Son of Man he not only identified himself as a human and as a special human, but he identified himself as one who can lead us to our destiny.

Aside from the expectations the Jewish people attached to the term "Son of Man," it simply means "man," humanity at its highest, its most exalted. Unfortunately, as a race, we fail to live up to that exalted possibility. I heard about a preacher who was called upon to officiate at the funeral of the town's outstanding rascal. Hard-pressed to say something good about the man he came up with this gem: "He wasn't as mean all the time as he was most of the time. It was the inconsistency in his pattern of meanness that gave him whatever claim to virtue that he had." Sometimes that's about as much as can be said for our virtues.

I remember a "Dear Abby" column from a few years ago. Someone wrote to advice columnist, Abigail Van Buren:

"Dear Abby, I'm single; I'm forty years old; I'd like to meet a man about the same age who has no bad habits."

Abby replied, "So would I."

Of course, this isn't a problem that only affects males. Anthropologist and writer Loren Eiseley explained it this way:

> Man is not completed—that is the secret of his paradoxical behavior. He is not made. He is, perhaps, about to be. Once long ago in the Middle Ages he was called *Homo duplex*—a thing half of dust and half of spirit. The term well-expresses his predicament. (www.positiveatheism.org/hist/eisely/htm. Credited to *The Saturday Evening Post*, "An Evolutionist Looks at Modern Man," circa 1959)

Our better side often gets lost. Jesus says, "The Son of Man came to seek out and to save the lost" (Luke 19:10). But to do that, he had to be one of us.

In March 1988, students at Gallaudet University in Washington, D.C., demonstrated the importance of having a leader who can identify with those who are led. Gallaudet is the nation's only all-deaf university. Professors must know sign language to teach there. In the second week of March the university trustees chose a new president. She was not deaf. She did not know sign language. She had her doctorate in nursing. The students were angry. They were deaf. They wanted a deaf president. They wanted someone who had walked where they walked, who could communicate with them and understand the unique needs of living quiet in a noisy world, someone who could be their hero. The students walked off campus and boycotted classes. By the end of the week the president-elect was gone, and a new president who had experienced the problems of the deaf was appointed. If we are to be led from where we are to where we are intended to be, it has to be by one who knows what it is like to be human.

A preacher was visiting the Sunday school kindergarten class. He asked the boys and girls if they would like to hear a story. They all said yes, and one little boy suggested, "Tell us a story about Andy."

"Well," the preacher said, "we don't use stories about Andy. We use stories about Jesus."

"No," the youngster persisted, "I want to hear about Andy."

"I don't understand," said the preacher. "Where did you get the name Andy?"

"You know," the boy said, "from the song: 'Andy walks with me, Andy talks with me, Andy tells me I am his own . . .'"

That Andy is indeed one whose story we can tell. He became like us. He called himself the Son of Man. And in his humanity we have a glimpse of what God intended us to be.

Old Testament Lesson

Daniel 7:13-14 (RSV)

I saw in the night visions,
and behold, with the clouds of heaven
    there came one like a son of man,
and he came to the Ancient of Days
    and was presented before him.

And to him was given dominion
    and glory and kingdom,
that all peoples, nations, and languages
    should serve him;
his dominion is an everlasting dominion,
    which shall not pass away,
and his kingdom one
    that shall not be destroyed.

New Testament Lesson

Matthew 16:13-28

Now when Jesus came into the district of Caesarea Philippi, he asked his disciples, "Who do people say that the Son of Man is?" And they said, "Some say John the Baptist, but others Elijah, and still others Jeremiah or one of the prophets." He said to them, "But who do you say that I am?" Simon Peter answered, "You are the Messiah, the Son of the living God." And Jesus answered him, "Blessed are you, Simon son of Jonah! For flesh and blood has not revealed this to you, but my Father in heaven. And I tell you, you are Peter, and on this rock I will build my church, and the gates of Hades will not prevail against it. I will give you the keys of the kingdom of heaven, and whatever you bind on earth will be bound in heaven, and whatever you loose on earth will be loosed in heaven." Then he sternly ordered the disciples not to tell anyone that he was the Messiah.

From that time on, Jesus began to show his disciples that he must go to Jerusalem and undergo great suffering at the hands of the elders and chief priests and scribes, and be killed, and on the third day be raised. And Peter took him aside and began to rebuke him, saying, "God forbid it, Lord! This must never happen to you." But he turned and said to Peter, "Get behind me, Satan! You are a stumbling block to me; for you are setting your mind not on divine things but on human things."

Then Jesus told his disciples, "If any want to become my followers, let them deny themselves and take up their cross and follow me. For those who want to save their life will lose it, and those who lose their life for my sake will find it. For what will it profit them if they gain the whole world but forfeit their life? Or what will they give in return for their life?

"For the Son of Man is to come with his angels in the glory of his Father, and then he will repay everyone for what has been done. Truly I tell you, there are some standing here who will not taste death before they see the Son of Man coming in his kingdom."

Suggested Hymns

- "Come, Thou Long Expected Jesus"
- "What Child Is This"
- "Lift Up Your Heads, Ye Mighty Gates"

Pastoral Prayer

Gracious and Loving God,

May the coming of Jesus Christ be experienced in our lives. Too often we treat him as a fictional hero or someone in a nice story, but his coming makes no impact on us or on our actions.

We spend our lives looking for something to which we can give our total allegiance: this loved one, that good cause, our family, our church, our nation. Inevitably, those humans and human institutions to which we give our allegiance get in the way of that primary allegiance for which we have been created. And invariably, those lesser loyalties disappoint us. Help us to give up our experimenting and to settle our allegiance on the one you have sent to guide and strengthen us, Jesus Christ. May we learn of him, and in learning find the one who will not disappoint. May his gentleness, goodness, and mercy be the foundation on which we build our lives. May his promise of life in your presence be the hope that sustains us and gives us direction. We pray in his name. Amen.

Litany for Lighting the Second Advent Candle

The season of Advent continues.
God comes among us in many ways.
We remember God's coming in Emmanuel:
God with us.

The First Advent Candle Is Lit.

From of old people of faith have looked for one like a Son of Man.
Jesus became the Son of Man to show us what God intended us to be.
May his life be our light.

The Second Advent Candle Is Lit.

Let us join our voices in singing the first verse of "O Young and Fearless Prophet."

Third Sunday of Advent

Ways We Know Him: Example

Scriptures: Matthew 9:35-36; Luke 23:33-34; John 13:1-5, 12-17

Sermon

Theodore Roosevelt once confessed that when he had a difficult decision to make he used to look at a large painting of Abraham Lincoln that hung above his desk and ask himself: "What would Lincoln do if he were in my shoes?" (as reported by Dale Carnegie in *How to Win Friends and Influence People* [Simon and Schuster, 1981], 40). For Roosevelt, Lincoln was an example. Example is an important way to teach. Albert Schweitzer testified to that when he said, "Example is not the *main* thing in influencing others. It is the *only* thing." Then he demonstrated that he believed it by following the example of Christ in a mission of healing in Africa.

Jesus fulfills many roles for those who seek to follow him: Messiah, Special Human, Teacher. In addition to these things, he is also someone eminently worth following, an original worth copying, a good example. To help us to understand the kind of example that Jesus set for us, I invite you to look with me at several things he did.

An Example of Compassion

For one thing, he demonstrated compassion. The word compassion is formulated from two words that mean to "suffer with." Throughout his ministry Jesus involved himself in the sufferings of others. In the passage from Matthew 9, Jesus is described as being moved with compassion for the masses because they were harassed and helpless, like sheep without a shepherd. In compassion he fed the hungry, healed the sick, taught the ignorant. He put his hand out and touched lepers. Even Sunday school children know the shortest verse in the Bible: "Jesus wept" (John 11:35 NIV)—words that remind us that Jesus entered into the sorrows of others.

If we want to follow Jesus' example, we too need to come to the point where we feel the pain of others. A woman and her husband interrupted their vacation to go to a dentist.

"I want a tooth pulled, and I don't want gas because I'm in a big hurry," the woman said, "so just extract the tooth as quickly as possible and we'll be on our way."

The dentist was quite impressed and said, "You're certainly a courageous woman. Which tooth is it?"

The woman turned to her husband and said, "Show him your tooth, dear."

How easy it is to call the shots when you don't feel the pain. Compassion calls for more than that.

And fortunately, most people are capable of more compassion than that. Mencius was a Chinese philosopher who lived several hundred years before Christ. Eager to show that there is good in everyone, he said,

> No man is devoid of a sensitivity to the suffering of others ... Suppose a man were, all of a sudden, to see a young child on the verge of falling into a well. He would certainly be moved to compassion, not because he wanted to get in the good graces of the parents, nor because he wished to win the praise of his villagers or friends, nor yet because he disliked the cry of the child. (*Mencius*, II.A.6 as translated by D.C. Lau, 1970)

Mencius was right. Most people do have a capacity for compassion.

And following Christ tends to heighten people's awareness of that characteristic. Flannery O'Connor, the insightful Roman Catholic writer, lifted up the Christian dimension when she said that people find Christ when they are concerned with other people's sufferings rather than their own.

An Example of Action

The example of Christ, however, demonstrates that it is not enough to feel simply compassionate for someone we also need to act. In Albert Camus' novel, *The Fall*, an established, impeccable French lawyer has his world totally under control until one night when he hears a drowning woman's cry and he turns away. Years later, ruined by guilt for his failure to act, he is found carrying on a conversation himself in an Amsterdam bar. First he imagines a prosecutor condemning him for his cowardliness. Then his conscience pleads with the young woman to throw herself into the water again so that he might have the chance to save not only her, but himself.

God binds us together in one family. Compassion calls us to enter into each other's suffering and share it. In the fall of 1989, Lamar Consolidated High School in Rosenburg, Texas, had nine students on campus with bald heads. It was a time when shaved heads weren't cool. The fellows weren't members of a political group or a religious cult. They were helping to bear the burden of a friend. When football player Lance O'Pry underwent surgery for cancer and started chemotherapy treatments, it was inevitable that he would lose his hair. A group of his friends and football teammates decided to show their solidarity with him by shaving their heads. They explained later that if Lance had to go through the experience of losing his hair, they were going to go through it too. That was compassion put into action.

Further, by his actions, Jesus demonstrated the importance of service. In the passage from John 13 that we read this morning, we heard how Jesus washed the feet of his disciples. He did not just say that serving others is important; he got down on his knees and did it. He fulfilled the role that would have normally fallen to a servant.

If we follow his example, we need to be aware that not all of those we serve are going to be grateful, or even changed, by what we do. Judas Iscariot was still present when Jesus washed his disciples' feet, yet he went out and betrayed Jesus. A church I am acquainted with sponsored a refugee family, setting them up in a house, securing a car, and helping to pay their bills. Subsequently, the refugee family cheated the church out of a large sum of money and ran off with the furniture. Some of the church members were naturally incensed and felt like never helping anyone again. They had to be reminded that service doesn't always engender gratitude, and that people shouldn't be surprised when the needy turn out to be sinners like everyone else. Being needy, of itself, does not necessarily make people noble.

In the Broadway musical, *Camelot*, the king describes his city as a place where there is no rain or fog in the daytime, where the snow never becomes a slushy mess, and where every evening is graced by moonlight.

It would be great to live in Camelot. Surely, there the needy would be nice. The hearts of those who serve would be warmed by smiles from thankful eyes. But Camelot does not exist. We are called to live and serve in an imperfect world where the poor are not perfect, the needy are not always nice, and where server and served alike are sinners.

Our reason for serving others, then, is not to make them grateful, but to show love by providing something that someone else needs. Those we serve may not always be loveable, but then neither are we. We serve others because we have received benefits, because we have something to share, and because it needs to be passed on.

Whether we change those we serve or not, serving has a profound impact on those offering the service. A reporter once asked the noted psychiatrist Dr. Karl Menninger: "Suppose a person felt a nervous breakdown coming on. What should he do?" You might have expected the mental health doctor to say, "See a psychiatrist." But he didn't. Instead, he advised: "Go straight to the front door, turn the knob, lock up your house, go across the railway tracks, find someone in need, and do something to help that person" (http://www.menningerclinic.com/about/early-history.htm).

The Indian writer Rabindranath Tagore, raised in a different culture from our own, described his discovery of this truth as a dream in which he imagined that life was to be all joy. When he awoke he discovered that life was really service and that service was joy.

Joseph Dutton is an American Catholic hero who, after years of alcoholism, spiritual struggles, and disappointment in marriage, gave his life to Christ and to the Catholic Church. He traveled widely seeking areas of ministry and finally settled and lived out his life on the island of Molokai in service to the lepers colonized there. Through faith he brought self-respect, calm, and joy to hundreds despite the awfulness of their illness. In time, the President of the United States wrote to him to compliment all that he had done on Molokai. Brother Dutton said that he could not understand the tribute. He was simply doing what had to be done and what he was able to do.

While not many of us can travel widely looking for places to minister, we should be aware that we do not have to. We have opportunity to minister to those close by, to our families, to our neighbors, to those in our community.

An Example of Forgiveness

One further characteristic that Jesus demonstrates is forgiveness. In the passage from Luke 23, we read how, on the cross, Jesus asked God to forgive his crucifiers. He had taught earlier that we are to pray for those who persecute us. Now he demonstrated it in his own conduct.

When we nurture animosity, it diminishes our own life. Gilbert and Sullivan were two giants in the field of light opera, but they couldn't control their tempers. Sullivan ordered new carpet for a theater they had purchased. When Gilbert saw the bill, he hit the roof. They battled it out in court, and never spoke to one another again as long as they lived. When Sullivan wrote the music for new productions, he would mail it to Gilbert, and when Gilbert wrote the words, he would mail them back to Sullivan. Once they had to make a curtain call together, but they stood on opposite sides of the stage so they wouldn't see each other. What a tragic waste of the friendship that could have enriched their lives.

There is a familiar story about a man who was wearing a heavy overcoat on a hot day. When a friend asked him why he was doing that, he replied, "Because it feels so good when I take it off." Some of us are walking around in great discomfort because we won't get rid of a burdensome grudge. We refuse to forgive someone who has wronged us. Most of us have enough to deal with in life without carrying around a heavy mantle of bad feelings, grudges, or lust for revenge. These really turn out to be forms of self-punishment that cost us far more dearly than they cost the person with whom we are at odds.

It is forgiveness that saves us from our own self-imposed hell. In his book, *How Can It Be All Right When Everything Is All Wrong* (New York: Simon & Schuster, 1982, 51–3), Lewis Smedes notes several characteristics of forgiveness. "Forgiveness is not forgetting," he says. We forget things that do not matter to us; " . . . forgiveness is remembering and still forgiving."

Neither, says Smedes, is forgiving excusing. Excusing is a product of understanding all the circumstances that made a situation what it was, so that the offender's personal responsibility is diminished. Excusing "is a way of telling a person that he does not really need to be forgiven after all."

According to Smedes, forgiveness *is* starting over and trying again with a person who has caused us pain. "It does not always take away the hurt. It does not deny the past injury. It merely refuses to let it stand in the way of a new start." It is holding out your hand and saying, "I want to be your friend again."

When a deep injury has been done to us, we don't recover until we forgive. Those who were held hostage in Lebanon some years ago discovered that. If any people ever had a right to hold a grudge, to harbor resentment, it is they. Yet each of them indicated a need to forgive their captors, so that their horrible captivity could be put behind them, so that they could get on with their lives.

The writer, Alex Noble, describes his discovery of the redemptive effect of forgiveness:

> Yesterday I decided to make a list of everyone in my life that I felt had been unjust or unkind to me. I started the list, and keep adding to it. As each name comes to my thought, I offer a gift of complete forgiveness. Not just for now, but for always. This exercise is taking on the atmosphere of a celebration: friendships restored to their original splendor, grievances healed, debts paid, feuds settled, disputes cancelled . . . What more important transformation can there be than to discover a friend where I had seen an enemy? To let the spirit of forgiveness transform my dragons into angels. (as quoted in *Pulpit Resources*, vol. 9, Third Quarter, Year A [Byron, Calif.: Pulpit Resource, Inc., 1981], 38)

Transforming dragons into angels—that is what Jesus was doing when, from the cross, he cried, "Father, forgive them."

A Great Teacher

Someone once said, "A mediocre teacher tells, a good teacher explains, a superior teacher demonstrates; but the great teacher inspires." Last week we looked at some of the things Jesus taught. Today we have seen how his words and example had a consistency about them that makes him eminently worth following. It is not enough, however, to remember that Jesus had compassion, that Jesus served, and that Jesus forgave. He came to provide us with an example of the kind of life God calls forth in all his children. His example makes a difference in your world only if it makes a difference in you.

Gospel Lessons

Matthew 9:35-36

Then Jesus went about all the cities and villages, teaching in their synagogues, and proclaiming the good news of the kingdom, and curing every disease and every sickness. When he saw the crowds, he had compassion for them, because they were harassed and helpless, like sheep without a shepherd.

Luke 23:33-34

When they came to the place that is called The Skull, they crucified Jesus there with the criminals, one on his right and one on his left. Then Jesus said, "Father, forgive them; for they do not know what they are doing." And they cast lots to divide his clothing.

John 13:1-5, 12-17

Now before the festival of the Passover, Jesus knew that his hour had come to depart from this world and go to the Father.

Having loved his own who were in the world, he loved them to the end. The devil had already put it into the heart of Judas son of Simon Iscariot to betray him. And during supper Jesus, knowing that the Father had given all things into his hands, and that he had come from God and was going to God, got up from the table, took off his outer robe, and tied a towel around himself. Then he poured water into a basin and began to wash the disciples' feet and to wipe them with the towel that was tied around him.

. . . .

After he had washed their feet, had put on his robe, and had returned to the table, he said to them, "Do you know what I have done to you? You call me Teacher and Lord—and you are right, for that is what I am. So if I, your Lord and Teacher, have washed your feet, you also ought to wash one another's feet. For I have set you an example, that you also should do as I have done to you. Very truly, I tell you, servants are not greater than their master, nor are messengers greater than the one who sent them. If you know these things, you are blessed if you do them."

Suggested Hymns

- "O Little Town of Bethlehem"
- "I Want to Walk as a Child of the Light"
- "O Master, Let Me Walk with Thee"

Pastoral Prayer

Christmas will come upon us shortly, and most of us find that we are not ready. It is not that we haven't gotten to all the baking, shopping, wrapping, and mailing that we intended to do, though that is part of the problem. We are not ready precisely because we have been taking care of these things.

We have many places to go and all kinds of festivities to enter into, and it is these things that prevent us from thinking about what the coming of Jesus should mean in our everyday life.

We celebrate a birthday, but give little thought to the one whose birth is celebrated.

Then, too, there are concerns that dampen the spirit a bit and make us wonder what the future holds. There is conflict and chaos in distant lands and threats of violence at home. Your call to peace and goodwill just hasn't gotten through to the world. But then, perhaps we are expecting too much.

How can we expect the spirit that was in Jesus to make any difference in the world if we have not got the time to let it make any difference in us?

May these moments of worship this morning cause us to pause and reflect on whether that child born in Bethlehem so long ago has really been born in us. And if he has, how shall we express it, not just at Christmastime, but all the time? Lord, help us to be such disciples of Christ that the world may not only see Christ in us, but come to believe in him. In the name of Christ we pray. Amen.

Litany for Lighting the Third Advent Candle

Christ comes among us in many ways.

He comes among us as Emmanuel
and assures us that God is with us.

The First Advent Candle Is Lit.

He calls himself the Son of Man.

He identifies with our humanity
and shows us our destiny.

The Second Advent Candle Is Lit.

He sets an example for how we are to live.
He challenges us to live lives marked by compassion, service, and forgiveness.

The Third Advent Candle Is Lit.

Let us join our voices in singing the fourth verse of "Lord, I Want to Be a Christian."

Fourth Sunday of Advent

Ways We Know Him: Lord

Scripture: Philippians 2:1-11

Sermon

There is a story that Satan once brought together his leading henchmen to map out a strategy against the church. Satan stood at the blackboard charting out a game plan, describing the demonic warfare in which they would be involved. At the close of the session Satan said, "Now get out there and give your best possible effort to keep those Christians from winning the lost." As his hellish henchmen headed for the door, Satan yelled after them; "By the way, be careful. If those Christians ever begin to really believe what they say and act on it, then hell help us, all heaven is going to break loose." If Christians took seriously the things which they say...

From earliest times Christians have called Jesus "Lord." In the early days of the church the Roman Empire decreed that every person was required to go to a temple each year and say, "Caesar is Lord." Many Christians could not and would not do that, because for them there could be only one Lord, and that was

Jesus. As a consequence, many suffered for what they believed. In spite of that, the church grew.

Today, in congregations like ours, across the church, Christians rise to recite the Apostles' Creed, which states that Jesus is Lord, but nothing happens; the church does not grow. We have the words, but we do not experience the commitment. A young man named John was sitting on the couch watching television with his girlfriend. He reached out, put his arm around her, and said, "I adore you, I need you, I can't live without you, I love you." The girl pushed him aside and said, "Oh John, I don't want to get serious." To which John replied, "Who's serious?"

What I want to suggest is that we get serious about what it means to call Jesus "Lord." To help you do that for yourself I would like to share what that statement means to me.

Lord of My Mind

The first thing I want to say is that for me to call Jesus "Lord" means that he is Lord of my mind. But that does not mean that, because I am a person of faith, I cease to think. I can remember that when I was in the sixth grade I learned some fascinating things about the development of life on this planet. We were taught that life had been developing for a long time, and that hundreds of thousands of years ago there had been some rather strange-looking people who lived in caves. I even produced a little play about two kinds of prehistoric people. A friend and I spent a lot of time making a saber-tooth tiger. When I went to Sunday school and told them what I had learned, the information was coolly received. In fact, several weeks later we had a film in Sunday school that contrasted a gargantuan ape-man with a Mel Gibson-type Adam, and we were asked to choose which of these was more likely the kind of human whom the Bible described as being made in God's image. I opted for the Mel Gibson-type, in spite of what I had learned in school. I didn't know it then, but I was being conditioned to think that in any showdown between worldly knowledge and my church's interpretation of the Bible, the Bible must be the ultimate authority, regardless of the field. I discovered that, though our home in this solar system may be called a universe, a place where one law governs, in reality, there were two kinds of truth—scientific truth and religious truth—and they often didn't come out at the same place! I hasten to say that that church was in a different denomination. I went through the first couple of years of college trying to preserve that dichotomy, putting faith over here and reason over there, trying to learn from professors, and yet having the conviction that when it came right down to what mattered, they didn't have the truth, and I did.

But somewhere along the way a change took place. My mind could not tolerate the inconsistency between what the school taught and what that church expected. I discovered for myself that I could use my mind without abandoning my faith. However, in the process I did have to adjust my ideas of what the faith was. As a result, the faith became my faith, not someone else's.

For Christians to say that Jesus is Lord of our minds does not mean, therefore, that we cease to use our minds. I acknowledge that sometimes the church has discouraged thinking and suggested that some thoughts are unthinkable. Sometimes the church has been afraid of thinking for fear of where it might lead. For that reason the Roman Church has had an "Index" on which it placed books that Catholics were forbidden to read, not because they were pornographic or immoral, but because they proposed disturbing thoughts; as though one could suppress what is called "error" by refusing to deal with it openly. One of the most creative writers in the Roman Church in recent years was a French priest, a world-renowned paleontologist, by the name of Pierre Tielhard de Chardin, whose writings propose fascinating things about the future of humanity. Unfortunately, his superiors refused to let him publish his works while he was alive. His works were only published after his death because friends defied the ban, and as a consequence, science and faith have been enriched by his writings.

Sometimes Christian people have been afraid of thinking any new thought because they are afraid that if they get all the pieces out of the box, they will never get them all back in again, and things won't ever again be just the way they were. Perhaps they shouldn't be just the way they were . . .

In The United Methodist Church we are taught that there are a number of ways in which we arrive at what is to be believed: through the Bible, personal experience, the traditions of the church, and reason. Therefore, we must not be afraid to think, and to let others think, for we will find that the Lord is gracious and ready to reveal himself to those of an enquiring mind. To call Jesus "Lord" does not require leaving our minds behind, for when Jesus was asked, "What is the greatest commandment?" he replied, "You shall love the Lord your God with all your heart, and with all your soul, and with all your mind" (Matthew 22:37).

Lord of My Heart

The second thing it means to me when I say, "Jesus is Lord," is that he is not only Lord of my mind, but of my heart as well. All human beings have something at the center of their lives.

Someone once said that there is a God-shaped place in the heart of each of us, where it is intended that God should be. In the lives of many persons that place is empty, and it makes the person feel empty. Or it may be filled with something that ought not to be there, and when something happens to that object, the person is completely devastated: it may be a human being whom we love, and who lets us down; it may be material advancement, and when we lose those material things, we feel the world has caved in. Most commonly, however, it is ourselves. This is humanity's most universal problem: self-centeredness. Right and wrong, good and bad, justice and truth all become subject to whether they advance or retard our own interest—and that is what it means to be a sinner.

Sometimes God does make it to the central place in our lives, but the place we are willing to make available to God is small and restricted. Wilbur Rees speaks for many people when he says,

> I would like to buy $3.00 worth of God, please, not enough to explode my soul or disturb my sleep, but just enough to equal a cup of warm milk, or a snooze in the sunshine. I don't want enough of Him to make me love a black man or make me pick beets with a migrant. I want ecstasy, not transformation; I want the warmth of the womb, not new birth. I want a pound of the eternal in a paper sack. I would like to buy $3.00 worth of God, please. (Wilber Rees, "$3.00 Worth of God" [Judson Press, 1971] in *When I Relax I Feel Guilty* by Tim Hansel [David C. Cook Publishing Company, 1979], 49)

To restrict the role of God in our lives is to acknowledge that something else is still Lord.

My understanding of the Christian faith is that a Christian is one who has made a decision to follow Jesus Christ. That decision may be called by many names. Some say they have "been saved." Others say they have been "converted," or "born again," or "found God," or "accepted Christ," or had a "Christian experience." But following any of these experiences there needs to be a growing commitment by the individual of his or her life to the kind of God revealed by Jesus Christ.

As told in James Dobson's *Emotions: Can You Trust Them?* (Ventura, Calif.: Regal Books, 1980), Everett Howard, a missionary to the Cape Verde Islands, tells how that commitment came about in his life. As a young man, he had come to a point in his life where he wanted to turn his life over to God. He locked himself in a little church, knelt down at the altar, took out a piece of paper, and filled it with promises he was willing to make to God. He listed everything he thought God might want of him. Then he signed his name and laid the sheet on the altar. He expected some kind of dramatic expression of gratitude by God. Nothing happened. Disappointed, he added more things. Still nothing. After a long silence, he felt that the voice of God was speaking to him, telling him to tear up the paper. Then the voice told him to sign a blank piece of paper and let God fill it in. He said that he did what he was told, and he reported thirty-six years later that God had been filling it in every day. Howard reported that he was glad he didn't know what was going to be written on the page: missionary service, illness, famine, or privation. Looking back, he said, those were days of blessing because God was there. And if he could turn around and do it again he would still let God fill in the page.

I cannot say that I have come to such a level of commitment in my life, but I do believe that is the direction in which we are led when we make Jesus the Lord of our hearts.

Lord of My Actions

The third thing that I want to say today is that when I say, "Jesus is Lord," it means to me that he is not only Lord of my mind and heart, but Lord of my actions as well. Too much religion is expressed by words, as though to say the right thing is to be the right thing. But, alas, we can confess with our lips and deny with our lives. Somewhere I read of an encounter that Mark Twain had with a man who managed to combine the appearance of piety with an unscrupulous career in business.

> "Before I die, I mean to make a pilgrimage to the Holy Land," a nineteenth-century industrial baron once said to Mark Twain. "I will climb to the top of Mount Sinai and read the Ten Commandments aloud."
>
> "Why don't you stay home and keep them," replied Twain. (as quoted in Brian Cavanaugh, *The Sower's Seeds* [Mahwah, N. J.: Paulist Press, 2004], 55)

"Not everyone who says to me, 'Lord, Lord,' will enter the kingdom of heaven," says Jesus, "but only the one who does the will of my Father in heaven" (Matthew 7:21).

Jesus teaches us about the will of the Father. But it is precisely here that Christians need to be careful. Devotion may become a substitute for action, so that those who gather in his name to learn about him may confuse learning with obedience. Somewhere I read the story of a man, nearly seventy years old, who was a student at Columbia University. In fact, he had spent almost fifty years as a student in that university. His father had stipulated in his will that his son was to receive a certain amount of money every month for as long as he was a student in college. So the man just stayed in school, taking every course that was offered. He learned a lot about many things and earned a number of degrees. He probably was one of the most educated men of his day. But who can say that such a life was a success? The purpose of going to school is to equip a person to go out into life and live the things one has learned. To be devoted to Jesus Christ, to learn from him, but to do nothing with what we have learned—that is to deny him.

I have to confess that my actions often fall short of what I would like them to be. Though I seek to be a follower of Jesus Christ, there is still plenty of the old, self-serving me left. Sometimes I manage to do the right thing for the wrong reasons. Sometimes I do the wrong things because of ignorance or willfulness. But the great part about being a follower of Jesus Christ is that mistakes are allowed. Several years ago I went to a meeting in one of our neighboring churches. Many people had made banners celebrating the Christian faith. One that was meaningful to me read, "You are free today to fail." That is the meaning of grace: we are free today to fail, but not free not to try.

Grace Sufficient for My Deficiencies

I close with this thought. At a UCLA basketball game I attended awhile back, I saw the team trying hard to implement the instructions they had been receiving all season. Periodically, the coach would call time out and one could see him giving a very animated instructions to the players. Still, they continued to make mistakes and wound up behind at the end of the first half. After the half-time break, the team came back out on the court and went on to win. They were finally playing the coach's way. When I think of Jesus as "Lord" I think of him as the coach of my team. I have signed on because I want to be under his tutelage.

He teaches me how to play the game—the rules as well as the best plays. When I get the ball, hopefully I will play it the way he has taught me to play. Sometimes I fumble, because I am still learning, but he doesn't kick me off the team. His grace is sufficient for my deficiencies. And it can be the same for you. How about it, can Jesus count on you to be on his team?

New Testament Lesson

Philippians 2:1-11

If then there is any encouragement in Christ, any consolation from love, any sharing in the Spirit, any compassion and sympathy, make my joy complete: be of the same mind, having the same love, being in full accord and of one mind. Do nothing from selfish ambition or conceit, but in humility regard others as better than yourselves. Let each of you look not to your own interests, but to the interests of others. Let the same mind be in you that was in Christ Jesus, who, though he was in the form of God, did not regard equality with God as something to be exploited, but emptied himself, taking the form of a slave, being born in human likeness. And being found in human form, he humbled himself and became obedient to the point of death—even death on a cross. Therefore God also highly exalted him and gave him the name that is above every name, so that at the name of Jesus every knee should bend, in heaven and on earth and under the earth, and every tongue should confess that Jesus Christ is Lord, to the glory of God the Father.

Suggested Hymns

- "Angels We Have Heard on High"
- "Fairest Lord Jesus"
- "It Came Upon the Midnight Clear"

Pastoral Prayer

Eternal God,

We find ourselves caught now in a period of preparation. In the language of the church it is Advent, and we acknowledge that this should be a time of spiritual preparation, reflection, and meditation so that the celebration of Christ's coming may be a meaningful high point in our lives. But who has time for reflection and meditation? It sounds good. It should be that way in our lives, but we are caught up in the realities. There are purchases to be made, gifts to be wrapped, baking to be done, a house to be prepared, planning menus, packing to go somewhere, or making rooms ready for people who will visit us, trying to make Christmas pleasant for others. But what about us? Don't we deserve to have it pleasant, too? We don't need hours of silence as though we were monks in a monastery, but we do need an opportunity to slow down and enjoy the season before it is gone. Important as it is to make memories for others, we need to have some time to recall our own memories and to reflect on them, whether they are painful or pleasant, for they have gone into the mix that makes us what we are. Reflection! That is what we need, Lord. And in our reflection, help us focus on the One who was born, and lived and died, and rose again to be the Lord of life. We pray in his name. Amen.

Litany for Lighting the Fourth Advent Candle

Christ comes to assure us of God's presence,
    to remind us that we are God's children,
    and to set an example for how we are to live.

He comes among us to show us the way.

The First Three Advent Candles Are Lit.

Many persons and causes demand our allegiance.
Jesus comes to us as the Lord of Life.
He is the one who deserves our highest loyalty.
May our hearts, minds, and actions serve his cause.

The Fourth Advent Candle Is Lit.

Let us join our voices in singing "He Is Lord."

Christmas Eve

Ways We Know Him: Son of God

Scripture: Galatians 4:1-7

Sermon

When I was a small boy, my older brother got an electric train for Christmas. He set it up in the living room and gave strict orders that I was not to play with it. Of course, when I was home alone, I couldn't resist the temptation. I ran the train too fast and it derailed. I stood over it trying to get all the wheels back on the track, but the wheels were loosely attached and kept going every which way. I couldn't get all of them back on track at the same time. My mother came home and observed what I was doing. "You can't do that from above," she said. "You have to get down beside it." Then she lay down on the floor where she could see to place the train back on its track. Somebody had to get down to where the problem was in order to fix it.

This is what happened when Christ came among us in that stable in Bethlehem. The human race had derailed and needed to be put back on the track of God's intention for our lives. God came down in the person of Jesus of Nazareth to live among us and show us how to get our lives back on track.

In the passage from Galatians, the apostle Paul focuses on the coming of Christ as an event that happened a long time ago, when the time was right. And, of course, the time was right. Alexander's conquests had given the whole known world one language: Greek. Roman legions had brought an enforced peace and built roads, making it easy to disseminate new ideas. Jewish religion was expectant, and pagan religion lacked moral fiber.

No wonder Paul speaks of the fullness of time, a time when many factors were converging to make this the right time for God to act. But Paul does not leave us with our attention focused only on an event in a manger so long ago, for the child born in a manger did not stay there. He grew up, taught, lived, died, rose again, and bestowed his spirit to empower his followers. In the passage, Paul uses several words to describe the human condition and the impact that Christ's coming has made on that condition.

Heirs of God

First, Paul describes us as heirs of God. Heirs are people who have a bright future. Unfortunately, it is possible to be an heir, but at the present moment, to be out of funds. If the desires of heirs get the best of them and they just have to have something right now, there are those who will accommodate them. I see advertisements every Sunday in the classified section of the newspaper appealing to just such people: "Heirs, you don't have to wait; we'll help you get what you want right now." Only I'm afraid that when the inheritance does come in, it will turn out to be a lot less because others will have acquired considerable interest in it. We can squander our inheritance.

Each year there are inheritances that go begging because people do not know that they are heirs. They need someone to tell them. So, Paul says in another place that we are "heirs of God, and joint heirs with Christ" (Romans 8:17). Of course, Paul has a deeper message in mind than the inheritance of wealth. He is saying that our destiny, individually and as the human race, is tied up with God. If people do not know that, they may be living spiritually impoverished lives needlessly.

Another thing about heirs is that for a time they may have to be under a guardian. Heirs, who may have title to a whole estate, may nevertheless be under the control of others while they are young. For example, one might be under the direction of a governess. It is said that when Queen Victoria's heir-apparent, Albert Edward, was a child, he rebelled against the authority of his governess, insisting that she had no right to order him about since he was heir to the throne. Prince Albert, his father, came to him and read him this passage of scripture to point out that even an heir must be subject for a time.

All of us who raise children are aware that children must be guided until they are old enough to think for themselves. Children are disciplined while they are young so that, when they are old enough to make decisions for themselves, they will have learned that they can't do just as they please. I was talking with a young child the other day who told me that the only thing he liked about going to school was recess. All the rest of the time they wanted him to do things he did not want to do; it was more fun to play. For his own good he has to be required to do things that he doesn't want to do until he learns to internalize the kind of conduct that brings good results. That is why there are laws to indicate right and wrong conduct, says Paul. The intention of the rules is to guide our conduct until we come to a level of maturity where we do the right thing because we want to. Though we were intended to live as children of God, all of us, like rebellious teenagers, have cut ourselves off from the Father, and have tried to live life on our own, generally with unsatisfactory results.

"Slaves" of God

Therefore, the next word Paul uses as he refers to us is "slaves." Desiring freedom, children will often throw off the very restraints intended to bring them to maturity. I know a young girl who, at fifteen years of age, got tired of her parents' direction. One evening she took the keys to the family car while her parents were away, and she went joyriding. She was involved in a terrible accident in which she suffered massive injuries, and she has now been in a vegetative state for years. So often, young people leave home, sometimes in a state of hostility, thinking they are ready for anything, only to forfeit their potential because they are not ready for what they encounter. They are still children.

I have been interested to notice that in recent years there have been several cases where children have divorced their parents. They are still the biological offspring of their parents—they still share the same genes—but the youngsters are saying, "I no longer wish to be known as your child."

It is such an attitude that Paul is addressing here. He is suggesting that we are like those children. We have rebelled against God, our Divine Parent, and forfeited our inheritance. Made to be God's children, to know God as companion and concerned parent, we choose instead to reject God's guidance, and it leads to separation.

But it doesn't stop there. Paul says that our childish rebellion leads us to become slaves, slaves to what Paul calls "the elemental spirits of the world" (Galatians 4:3) or "... of the universe" (Colossians 2:8). What Paul meant by "the elemental spirits" is open to debate. He may have meant "the elements," what the world is composed of. This would be an attitude of materialism, the assumption that *things* produce happiness.

It's interesting to watch children talk to Santa Claus, but it makes me uncomfortable when I hear Santa say, "And what do you want for Christmas, little girl?" The very question encourages a material attitude, and children respond to it with their long lists of wants. Parents buy into it, too, and reinforce it by the extreme efforts they are willing to make to secure the thing that will show their love for their child: waiting in line all night, for example, to be one of the first people to get into a store that is going to have only eleven highly-advertised dolls available for sale. We become captivated by things.

Perhaps Paul's phrase "elemental spirits of the universe" refers to the stars and planets, which were thought to control the destinies of individuals. Rebellious children, who no longer trust the good will of the Heavenly Parent, turn to all kinds of other strange devices and invest them with authority. By these manipulations, people hope to control their own destinies. Astrology, palmistry, card reading, fortune telling, and all kinds of occult activities are offered to a society that prefers to put its destiny in the hands of deified Chance, or Fate, or Fortune, rather than to live life trusting that God intends the best for us. What Paul is saying is that rebellious children, who cut themselves off from the one who made them for fellowship, are easy prey to all kinds of slavery.

God Sent His Son

The third word Paul uses in this passage is the word "son." "When the fullness of time had come," he says, "God sent his Son" (Galatians 4:4). What Paul means by "fullness of time" we have already seen. The time was right for a lot of reasons, but the most pressing reason was that the world was in need.

He says, "God sent." In Jesus, God was sending an emissary of reconciliation. In spite of all the previous setbacks, all the rebellion God had endured, from Adam on, God was willing to try again.

And what God sent, Paul says, was "God's Son." In the past there had been overtures from God in the form of spokespersons, like Moses, written statements, like the Ten Commandments, acts of atonement made by priests who offered sacrifice, but now God was sending a person who embodied God's Spirit to live among us.

For years Jacques Cousteau helped us to appreciate the beauty and mystery of nature. In his travels he came to appreciate the fact that families everywhere love their children. Therefore, during the cold war, he made a proposal, which, he was sure, would insure world peace. He suggested that there be a worldwide agreement that all the children of the world spend their seventh-grade school year as guests of a foreign country. With children widely distributed, they would have first-hand experience of how other people live, and at the same time, the students would serve as a guarantee that no nation would drop a bomb on another nation where their children were being hosted. In Jesus, God sent a son to live among us as a guarantee of God's good intentions toward humanity.

And the mission of the Son, Paul says, was to redeem us, to bring us back into God's family from whatever things have held us in bondage. I have heard that among the Cherokee Indians there was a law of capture and adoption. A soldier, traveling north with other white men from New Orleans, was captured by the Cherokees. A slave collar was placed around his neck. Not long afterward, the white soldier was bought by one of the Indians. Acting according to Cherokee custom, he was no longer a slave but was regarded as a brother or a cousin of the Indian who had purchased him. He was a slave before he was bought; he was an adopted brother after he was purchased. The whole tribe was required to treat him as another Indian. He was recognized as part of the tribe.

In the passage we have been looking at, Paul speaks of people becoming children of God by adoption. To be sure, God is the creator of the whole world and all living creatures. But to be God's child by adoption is a new and special relationship. Those who have been led to God through Jesus Christ have rescinded the divorce created by their rebellion and resumed the relationship for which they were made—to be children of God.

This is the good news that we celebrate at Christmas. This Son of God has come to restore us to our original relationship as the children of God we were intended to be. When Cyrus the Great was a baby, his grandfather, out of jealousy and fear that Cyrus would one day take the Persian throne from him, called a servant and charged him to take the baby away and destroy him. Instead of slaying the baby, the servant gave him to a childless shepherd living in a distant province. Cyrus grew up supposing that he was only a shepherd's son. One day he learned the truth, that he was a prince of the royal family and heir to the throne of Persia. From then on there was no tending the sheep for young Cyrus. He immediately began to fit himself to rule the kingdom, and eventually he did become king of Persia. The turning point came when he realized whose child he was, and that was the first step toward the fulfillment of his purpose in life. Jesus has come to tell us that we are children of God. We, too, have a heritage to claim.

To those who have forgotten how a child of God is supposed to act, Jesus provides an example. Michael B. Brown tells of an experience he had when he was the pulpit guest at a suburban church:

> I was approached by a member whom I had spotted during the second morning service. He had been sitting on the very front pew. He was a large man . . . not poorly dressed but did present a generally disheveled look, as if appearance were at the bottom of his list of personal priorities. All smiles, he approached me with a hug and the following greeting: "Hey, brother! All morning long people have been congratulating me on what a great sermon I preached at the 9:00 service. You and I must be twins." There were few things I wished to hear less. For months I had been involved in a rigorous program of exercise and had taken off 20 pounds. I try to dress appropriately for morning worship. And now to be mistaken for this fellow . . . I was not complimented. Later in the day, I mentioned the incident to my host pastor. He answered: "Yes, that's Willie. We call him 'Mr. Love' around here. He's all smiles. He knows everyone. He loves everyone, and it is certainly reciprocal. Willie is like a ray of sunshine to our church. He always greets newcomers in the halls. He escorts older persons to their cars after dark or in bad weather. He plays ball with our church kids. He regularly inquires about your homebound parents or sick aunt. He listens to people, prays with people, laughs, and even cries with people. He hugs everybody (at that point I recalled how he had greeted me that morning with a bear hug). Yes sir, that's Willie—our 'Mr. Love.'" And suddenly I found myself thinking: "If only my

> life could be that beautiful! If only I were worthy to be called his twin!" (Michael B. Brown, *Be All That You Can Be* [Lima, Ohio: CSS Publishing, 1995], 9–10)

How do children of God act? They act the way their brother, Jesus, has showed them. They act in love.

When the time was right, God sent his Son. We look back on that event, hallowed by all the Christmases that have ever been, and we are inclined to leave the event in Bethlehem with the manger, the star, the shepherds, and the wise men. But that would be a mistake, for what happened for those people two thousand years ago, also happened for us.

With the hymn writer, Phillips Brooks, we need to pray:

> O holy Child of Bethlehem,
> descend to us we pray;
> cast out our sin, and enter in,
> be born in us today.
> We hear the Christmas angels
> the great glad tidings tell;
> O come to us, abide with us,
> Our Lord Emmanuel.
> ("O Little Town of Bethlehem," stanza 4)

Old Testament Lesson

Isaiah 9:2, 6-7

> The people who walked in darkness
>   have seen a great light;
> those who lived in a land of deep darkness—
>   on them light has shined.
> . . . .

For a child has been born for us,
a son given to us;
authority rests upon his shoulders;
and he is named
Wonderful Counselor, Mighty God,
Everlasting Father, Prince of Peace.
His authority shall grow continually,
and there shall be endless peace
for the throne of David and his kingdom.
He will establish and uphold it
with justice and with righteousness
from this time onward and forevermore.
The zeal of the LORD of hosts will do this.

New Testament Lesson

Galatians 4:1-7

My point is this: heirs, as long as they are minors, are no better than slaves, though they are the owners of all the property; but they remain under guardians and trustees until the date set by the father. So with us; while we were minors, we were enslaved to the elemental spirits of the world. But when the fullness of time had come, God sent his Son, born of a woman, born under the law, in order to redeem those who were under the law, so that we might receive adoption as children. And because you are children, God has sent the Spirit of his Son into our hearts, crying, "Abba! Father!" So you are no longer a slave but a child, and if a child then also an heir, through God.

Suggested Hymns

- "O Come, All Ye Faithful"
- "Away in a Manger"
- "Silent Night"

Pastoral Prayer

Once again we have come to Christmas, Lord, and we find ourselves, as always, filled with nostalgia. Our feelings are not quite the same as they were when we were young and filled with anticipation. And yet, we are warmed by those memories accumulated over the years—memories that we would not give up, but that may also give us pain because things are different now. So, in this season of joy we find ourselves ambivalent, singing carols as we have always done, and yet a bit misty-eyed too. Perhaps occasions such as this always do that to us: we are glad for what they commemorate, but wistful about the past.

Help us, then, in the light of our maturity, have Christmas speak to us in a manner that may be different from the way it spoke to us as children, but still in a way that brings joy to our hearts. And help us share our perception with those of a different generation, so that their understanding of Christmas may be deepened, even as their joy and simplicity enrich us.

All of us will come to Christmas differently, Lord, and no one experience is all there is to it. But for every one of us may it be an affirmation that you love us and accept us, no matter what. We pray in the name of him who came to proclaim your love. Amen.

Litany for Lighting the Fifth Advent Candle

The Advent candles remind us that Christ is known
by many names.
This evening we again light the outer candles
of the Advent wreath to remind ourselves
that Christ is known to us as
Emmanuel, Son of Man, Example, and Lord.

The First Four Advent Candles Are Lit.

May our lives reflect his light in the world.
The center candle is the Christ candle.
Tonight we remember him as the Son of God.
"For God so loved the world
that he gave his only Son,
so that everyone who believes in him may not perish,
but have everlasting life."
As he was once born in Bethlehem,
may he be born also in the lives of each of us.

The Christ Candle Is Lit.

Let us join our voices in singing the fourth verse of
"O Little Town of Bethlehem."

Christmas Day

Ways We Know Him: Word of God

Scripture: John 1:1-18

Sermon

"Truly, you are a God who hides himself," cried Isaiah in exasperation (45:15). And many of us have felt the same. But in the New Testament, the writer of the letter to the Hebrews opens his letter with the confident assertion: "Long ago God spoke to our ancestors in many and various ways . . ." and the Bible does indeed appear to be a record of many of those revelations. The experience of the race has been ambiguous: some people have found God to be elusive; others have found God to be revealing. Perhaps the truth is that there are some things we don't want to know about God because to acknowledge them would require some response from us.

I read about a little girl who went to the library and asked the librarian to help her find a book about penguins. The librarian found a big book and sent it home with the girl. The next day the girl brought the book back. "Done already?" asked the librarian. "No," said the girl, "I brought it back because this book tells more about penguins than I want to know."

God sought Adam and Eve in the Garden of Eden, but they hid from God. God came to Jacob in a dream, but Jacob was not ready to give up his wily ways, and he fled to another land. God called Moses to go and save his people in Egypt, but Moses protested that he was not eloquent. Jonah was called to proclaim God's love to an enemy of his people, but Jonah boarded a ship headed in the opposite direction. Saul of Tarsus was confronted with the first Christian martyr, Stephen, who was willing to die for his faith, but Saul chose to deny that God was speaking to him.

It may be that God is not so much hidden as that we are reluctant to see God in various aspects of our lives. In the passage that we read today from the prologue of the Gospel of John, the writer refers to a number of ways in which God attempts to make God's self and God's will known to us.

God Revealed through Nature

John reminds us that one of the ways God reveals God's self to us is through nature. "All things came into being through him," says the writer in John 1:3. The Psalmist was prompted to say:

> When I look at your heavens, the work of your fingers,
> the moon and the stars that you have established;
> what are human beings that you are mindful of them?
> (Psalm 8:3-4)

And another psalm says, "The heavens are telling the glory of God; and the firmament proclaims his handiwork" (Psalm 19:1). I'm sure we have each had experiences that inspire similar awe: a magnificent sunset, a flight of migrating birds, the stillness of the desert at dusk, the fascination of a tide pool. Any of these things can make us pause long enough to look up in gratitude that we were allowed to be there.

And yet, nature, by itself, is often unable to draw us nearer to God. Even when we have sufficient insight to reflect on our experiences, they are usually of such variety that our conclusions are ambiguous. We are drawn to God by the beauty of the stars, but the coiling of a snake repels us. Our experiences are contradictory. We respond to some parts of God's creation, but other parts turn us away.

Some people, confronted with nature, don't find God there at all. In his book, *Cosmos*, astronomer Carl Sagan opts for a nontheological explanation of the origin of things. He writes:

> The idea that every organism was meticulously constructed by a Great Designer provided a significance and order to nature and an importance to human beings that we crave still. A Designer is a natural, appealing and altogether human explanation of the biological world. But, as Darwin and Wallace showed, there is another way, equally appealing, equally human, and far more compelling: natural selection, which makes the music of life more beautiful as the aeons pass. (Carl Sagan, *Cosmos* [New York: Random House, 1980], 29)

God can be found in nature, but we have to open our eyes and see it. Theodore Roethke wrote:

> For there *is* a God and He's here, immediate, accessible. I don't hold with those thinkers that believe that in this time God is farther way—that in the Middle Ages, for instance, He was closer. God is equally accessible now, not only in works of art or in the glories of a particular religious service, or in the light, the aftermath that follows the dark night of the soul, but in the lowest forms of life, He moves and has His being . . . Is this a

> new thought? Hardly. But it needs some practicing in Western society." (Ralph J. Mills Jr., Theodore Roethke, *On the Poet and His Craft* [University of Washington Press, 1965], 27)

Nature by itself doesn't get the message to everyone.

God Revealed through Reason

Another way John says that God reveals God's self to us is through reason. John speaks of the true light that enlightens everyone. I know that there are some religious groups that despise reason as an approach to God. For them, religion is a matter of faith, and the more unreasonable your beliefs are, the greater is your demonstration of faith. Consequently, some outrageous requirements are made in the name of religion, and faith becomes an attempt to believe the unbelievable. I am inclined to opt for reason as an approach to God, for it is with our minds that we pursue truth, and if God is truth, then one of our significant avenues of approach to God is our ability to think. Indeed, it is our ability to think that separates us from the animals, and may very likely be what is meant by "the image of God" in which we are made.

But reason, too, has its limitations as a revealer of God. Those who focus on reason often miss the spiritual side of life. The Princeton University faculty came up with this list of the ten biggest contributors to the advancement of human knowledge: Plato, Newton, da Vinci, Socrates, Aristotle, Darwin, Galileo, Shakespeare, Pasteur, Einstein. It seems strange that a Presbyterian school would omit the one name that has contributed the most to human understanding. Perhaps the learned faculty was distinguishing between scientific, literary knowledge and understanding, but even so it is a strange omission to leave off the name of Jesus, whose words of wisdom were an inspiration to most of the notables who made the Princeton list.

Blaise Pascal, the seventeenth century scientist, wrote: "The heart has its reasons that reason knows not of." He was suggesting that there is an emotional dimension to life that touches us in ways that reason does not.

Dr. Clement C. Moore was a divinity professor. He usually wrote theological treatises; he was especially fascinated with the incarnation and sought to explain the deeper meanings of the Christmas event. None of his theological expositions are remembered, however. But something he did write about Christmas is remembered. One Christmastime he saw an old Dutch gentleman with red cheeks and white hair smoking an old clay pipe, and all of a sudden he felt inspired to write a bit of verse for his children. So this theology professor went home after encountering this happy man and wrote for his children: " 'Twas the night before Christmas, when all through the house..." Dr. Moore thought his greatest influence would be as a theologian exploring the intellectual facets of Christmas, and it turned out that his greatest impact was when he let the emotions of Christmas work on him. It takes more than reason to help us find God.

God Revealed through Moral Law

God has also revealed God's self through moral law. John reminds us that Moses delivered the law of God. The understanding that there are moral laws that govern life is one of the significant contributions of Judaism. Indeed, Old Testament writers became positively rhapsodic about the effect of the law on life. The author of Psalm 19 wrote:

The law of the LORD is perfect,
    reviving the soul;
the decrees of the LORD are sure,
    making wise the simple;
the precepts of the LORD are right,
    rejoicing the heart;
. . . .
More to be desired are they than gold,
    even much fine gold;
sweeter also than honey,
    and drippings of the honeycomb. (Psalm 19:7-8, 10)

In other places the Psalmist says, "Oh, how I love your law!" (119:97). But experience with the law alone is not a satisfying one. Laws have a tendency to be preserved long after the reason for having them is forgotten.

Thomas Harris, in his book, *I'm Okay, You're Okay*, tells about a woman who related a parental edict that had long governed her household procedure. Her mother had told her, "Never put a hat on the table or a coat on the bed." So she went though life never putting a hat on the table or a coat on the bed. When occasionally she'd forget, there was overreaction. Finally, after living several decades with this unexamined law, the woman asked her mother, then in her eighties, "Mother, why do we never put a hat on a table or a coat on a bed?" Her mother replied that when she was little there had been some neighbor children who were infested with lice, and her mother had warned her that it was important to never put the neighbor children's hats on the table or their coats on the bed. The reason was gone; yet the edict was still in effect.

Laws also have a tendency to become negative. The editor of a local newspaper was interviewing an applicant for the job of rewrite man.

"Well," said the editor, "are you good?"

"Sure," was the reply.

"All right, then, fix this and cut it short," instructed the editor, handing him the Ten Commandments.

The applicant gave the copy a glance, seemed a little nonplussed, then stepped over to the desk and wrote briefly.

He handed it to the editor, who studied the paper for only a moment, then looked up and said, "You're hired." The rewrite on the paper was simply "Don't." When we concentrate on the laws, we miss the point, which is to please God.

God Revealed through Words

John also points out that God reveals God's self through words, for he reminds us of the testimony of John the Baptist. There is also the written word—the Bible. It is important because it brings to us the experiences of our Jewish forebears and of the early church. Some folks call the Bible the Word of God and they require slavish obedience to every word. Others of us would rather say that the Bible contains the Word of God in a human instrument, and therefore it needs to be interpreted and thoughtfully applied to each situation.

H.B. Tristram tells us how he once shared the Scriptures in Ceylon through an interpreter. As he later learned, he very unfortunately chose the parable of the lost sheep as his subject.

> My interpreter told me afterwards that not one of my hearers had ever seen a sheep or knew what it was. "How then," I asked, "did you explain what I said?" "Oh," he replied, "I

> turned it into a buffalo that had lost its calf and went into the jungle to find it." (*Eastern Customs in Bible Lands* [Kessinger Publishing, 2004], 117)

The spoken word can sometimes gets in the way of the message as well:

> W. B. J. Martin tells the story of an old missionary who had struggled by himself for many years. Finally, the mission board wrote to tell him that they had raised enough funds to send him an assistant. They sent him a young fellow who had just completed seminary and had all the self-confidence and certainty that comes with being young and being right out of seminary. When the young man arrived at the mission station they called together the chief and all the people of the tribe to welcome him. Then they asked the young missionary to say a few words. He could speak only in English, so the old missionary stood up to translate. The young fellow said something like this: "We must always remember that there is an infinite and qualitative distinction between the eternal gospel and all the historical manifestations of it under the contingencies of human existence."
>
> The old missionary just stood there for a moment, dumbfounded, as the young man waited for him to translate that. Finally, the wise old missionary turned to the people and said, "Friends, he says he loves you and he's glad to be here." (as quoted in *Pulpit Resources*, vol. 7 [Oxnard, Calif.: Pulpit Resource, Inc., 1979], 43)

God Revealed in the Living Word

Because of the inherent weaknesses in all these methods of revelation John says that God has revealed God's self in a living word. As John puts it in verse 14, "the Word became flesh . . ."

Several years ago, an atomic scientist was arguing for the value of exchange scholarships between nations. He was not thinking of Christmas, but he gave us a beautiful picture of Christmas when he said, "The best way to send an idea is to wrap it up in a person." That is what God did in the Incarnation: God took the idea of God's love and wrapped it up in the person of Jesus Christ. "The Word became flesh."

Søren Kierkegaard, the nineteenth-century Danish theologian, told a parable to illuminate what happened on that first Christmas. The parable speaks of a prince who saw a beautiful young woman while riding through the poorer section of town. Thereafter, he went out of his way to see her, and fell in love with her. He wanted to win her and make her his bride. He could force her to marry him, but he preferred that she marry him out of love, so he put on simple peasant clothes, moved into the neighborhood, and did the work of an ordinary workman. He adopted the language and concerns of the people among whom he lived. After the young woman came to know him and love him as he loved her, he revealed his true identity.

Kierkegaard was telling the Christmas story in another form. God loved the world and was looking for a way to win the world to himself. He could have ordered us to love him, but love cannot be commanded. So God became like us, taking on a human body and living among us. He told stories about God's love, and when some of us responded and returned God's love, God revealed who he was.

"The Word became flesh and lived among us, and we have seen his glory, the glory as of a father's only son, full of grace and truth" (John 1:14). From Jesus, we learn what God is like and that love is what ties us together as God's family (see John

Thomas Randolph, *The Best Gift* [Lima, Ohio: C. S. S. Publishing, 1983], 46–47). The parable is also known as "the king and the maiden" (see Søren Kierkegaard, *Philosophical Fragments* [Princeton: Princeton University Press, 1936]).

Old Testament Lesson

Exodus 33:17-23

The LORD said to Moses, "I will do the very thing that you have asked; for you have found favor in my sight, and I know you by name." Moses said, "Show me your glory, I pray." And he said, "I will make all my goodness pass before you, and will proclaim before you the name, 'The LORD'; and I will be gracious to whom I will be gracious, and will show mercy on whom I will show mercy. But," he said, "you cannot see my face; for no one shall see me and live." And the LORD continued, "See, there is a place by me where you shall stand on the rock; and while my glory passes by I will put you in a cleft of the rock, and I will cover you with my hand until I have passed by; then I will take away my hand, and you shall see my back; but my face shall not be seen."

New Testament Lesson

John 1:1-18

In the beginning was the Word, and the Word was with God, and the Word was God. He was in the beginning with God. All things came into being through him, and without him not one thing came into being. What has come into being in him was life, and the life was the light of all people. The light shines in the darkness, and the darkness did not overcome it.

There was a man sent from God, whose name was John. He came as a witness to testify to the light, so that all might believe through him. He himself was not the light, but he came to testify to the light. The true light, which enlightens everyone, was coming into the world.

He was in the world, and the world came into being through him; yet the world did not know him. He came to what was his own, and his own people did not accept him. But to all who received him, who believed in his name, he gave power to become children of God, who were born, not of blood or of the will of the flesh or of the will of man, but of God.

And the Word became flesh and lived among us, and we have seen his glory, the glory as of a father's only son, full of grace and truth. (John testified to him and cried out, "This was he of whom I said, 'He who comes after me ranks ahead of me because he was before me.' ") From his fullness we have all received, grace upon grace. The law indeed was given through Moses; grace and truth came through Jesus Christ. No one has ever seen God. It is God the only Son, who is close to the Father's heart, who has made him known.

Suggested Hymns

- "Joy to the World"
- "The First Noel"
- "Angels from the Realms of Glory"

Pastoral Prayer

Gracious God,

The day has arrived when people everywhere pause to recognize the birth of our lord. For many, it is a holiday, a festivity, a celebration that has little meaning beyond the lights and gifts because they do not know the Lord whose coming is celebrated.

We pray that those of us who do know him will demonstrate such a spirit of rejoicing that others will want to share what we have found here.

For others, the festivities are limited by hospitalization or confinement at home. Help those of us who are well to be mindful of those who are ill and to show compassion. There are those who are out of work, Lord, and worry about the future hangs heavy over them. May they receive as their gift the spirit of optimism and hopefulness. May they be blessed with the knowledge that Christmas is not found in the abundance of things we buy, but in loving one another—in sensing your love as it comes to us through people.

There are those who are lonely, and for whom the holiday hangs heavy, and whose only thought is to get through it as quickly as possible. Help all of us to be sensitive to the situations of others and to do what we can to enrich the lives of those who do not feel inclined to rejoice.

During the following moment of silence, help each of us gathered here in worship to focus on one person to whom you would have us bring a good word, or for whom you would have us perform some service.

(Silence)

Give us the determination that, when we leave this place, we will be able to perform what you are asking us to do. In the name of Christ we pray. Amen.

Advent Wreath Recognition

During the past weeks we have lit the five candles
of our Advent wreath.
They have reminded us of some of the ways
we know Christ.

Today the candles have already been lit to show
that Christ still manifests himself
in these and other ways.
What more is there to reveal?
He is called the Word of God.
May God help us to hear, to understand,
and to apply that Word in our own lives.
Let us join our voices in singing the first verse of
"Word of God Come Down to Earth."

Scripture Index